The House That Jack Built

A Mother Goose Rhyme
pictures by J. P. Miller

gb *Golden Press • New York*
Western Publishing Company, Inc.
Racine, Wisconsin

This is the house that Jack built.

This is the malt
That lay in the house
that Jack built.

This is the rat
That ate the malt
That lay in the house
    that Jack built.

This is the cat
That killed the rat
That ate the malt
That lay in the house
that Jack built.

This is the dog
That worried the cat
That killed the rat
That ate the malt
That lay in the house
that Jack built.

13

This is the cow
with the crumpled horn,

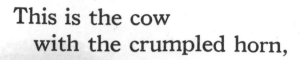

That tossed the dog

That worried the cat

That killed the rat

That ate the malt

That lay in the house
that Jack built.

This is the maiden
 all forlorn,
That milked the cow
 with the crumpled horn,
That tossed the dog
That worried the cat
That killed the rat
That ate the malt
That lay in the house
 that Jack built.

This is the man
  all tattered and torn,
That kissed the maiden
  all forlorn,
That milked the cow
  with the crumpled horn,
That tossed the dog
That worried the cat
That killed the rat
That ate the malt
That lay in the house
  that Jack built.

This is the priest
  all shaven and shorn,
That married the man
  all tattered and torn,
That kissed the maiden
  all forlorn,
That milked the cow
  with the crumpled horn,
That tossed the dog
That worried the cat
That killed the rat
That ate the malt
That lay in the house
  that Jack built.

This is the cock

that crowed

in the morn,

That waked the priest
all shaven and shorn,
That married the man
all tattered and torn,
That kissed the maiden
all forlorn,
That milked the cow
with the crumpled horn,
That tossed the dog
That worried the cat
That killed the rat
That ate the malt
That lay in the house
that Jack built.

This is the farmer
sowing his corn,

That kept the cock
   that crowed in the morn,
That waked the priest
   all shaven and shorn,
That married the man
   all tattered and torn,
That kissed the maiden
   all forlorn,
That milked the cow
   with the crumpled horn,
That tossed the dog
That worried the cat
That killed the rat
That ate the malt
That lay in the house
   that Jack built.

This is the horse and the hound and the horn,

That belonged to the farmer
sowing his corn,
That kept the cock
that crowed in the morn,
That waked the priest
all shaven and shorn.

That married the man
all tattered and torn,

That kissed the maiden
all forlorn,

That milked the cow
with the crumpled horn,

30

That tossed the dog

That worried the cat
That killed the rat
That ate the malt

That lay in the house that Jack built.